The Way of

THE DESERT

INTRODUCTION

The deserts of the world have a spirit all their own. These desolate, empty landscapes reach deep into the soul, eliciting a profound response. They are full of romance and danger. To think of the North African Sahara is to conjure images of slow Bedouin caravanserai winding their way over the dunes that rise and fall like waves on an endless sea of sand. To journey in the imagination to the vast outback of Australia is to take part in the Aboriginal dreamtime during which the primordial ancestors dreamed the world into existence, laying every sacred contour of each hill and valley. To step outside the bustle of the urban world into the American deserts is to be immersed in the mystery of solitude, which bares down on the soul like the burning sun.

The desert landscapes of the Middle East have inspired three of the great world religions – Judaism, Christianity, and Islam – as well as the ancient Egyptian religion, which illuminated the ancient Pagan world for more than five

Life's Daily
MEDITATIONS

TIMOTHY FREKE

Sterling Publishing Co., Inc.
New York

thousand years. Moses led his people across these deserts in search of the promised land. The early Christian "Desert Fathers" inhabited the tombs of dead pharaohs, desert caves, and solitary cells, where they lived as hermits

communing with God. Muhammad loved the deserts and mountains where he would go to meditate on Allah. It was here that he received visions of the angel Gabriel who dictated to him the Holy Koran, the sacred scripture of Islam. Islamic mystics, called Sufis, told stories about the desert to teach the faithful. Collectively they present a rich testament to the power of the desert to awaken the spiritual fire of the human imagination.

DESERT FEELINGS

 THE DESERT has many faces and evokes many feelings. It is a place whose awesome expanses speak of beauty, freedom, and death. To escape the power of the sun under the shadow of the pyramids or the sphinx is to be drawn back into the ancient world, when Ra the sun-god was worshiped morning and evening as he sailed his sky-boat across the heavens to delineate the day and night. To sky-watch on a desert night is to be over-awed by the population of shining stars, more numerous than the human beings that throng the cities, a still and silent contrast to our cacophony of business. For the Sufi poet Rumi a journey into the desert was a metaphor for the soul setting off into the Void of God. The caravanserai is ready to depart and the heavenly drum is sounding "let's go!"

Lovers, listen!

The time to leave this world has come.

My inner ear can hear

the heavenly drum sounding "let's go!".

Look! The camel driver is awake.

The camels are ready.

If you are a traveler,

why are you still sleeping?

Everywhere is the din of departure.

Each moment a soul is setting off into the Void.

You've fallen into a deep sleep;

as heavy as this life is light.

Soul, look for the Soul!

Friend, look for the Friend!

Watchmen should watch out, not doze off!

The streets are full of candles and torches,

clamor and confusion,

for tonight this changing world

gives birth to something eternal.

You were desert dust, but are now the wind.

You were foolish but are now made wise.

JALALUDIN RUMI

HYMN IN PRAISE OF
RA THE SUN-GOD

Blessings to You,

fierce fiery hawk,

as dreadful and beautiful as love.

Your light has burst upon the land,

like yellow pollen on a bee's back.

The gods are all singing,

intoxicated with your light.

It is Ra who gathers the world together,

springing from the formless water,

and taking the form of fire.

Like the first word,

he is uttered from the horizon's mouth.

Like music he passes through the heavens.

As long as the sun sings,

the strings of my lyre-like heart

vibrate a hymn in unison with him.

Until evening, may I walk under the sun,

forgetting time and reason.

May I explode with light,

like a purple flower of remembrance.

The air cracks and the sun beats its rhythm.

Everyday – the sun.

Everyday.

ANCIENT EGYPTIAN HYMN

O God, thou art my God; early will I seek thee;

my soul thirsteth for thee, my flesh longeth for thee

in a dry and thirsty land, where no water is;

To see thy power and thy glory,

so as I have seen these in the sanctuary.

Because thy loving kindness is better than life,

my lips shall praise thee.

Thus will I bless thee while I live:

I will lift up my hands in thy name.

My soul shall be satisfied as with marrow and fatness;

and my mouth shall praise thee with joyful lips:

When I remember thee upon my bed,

and meditate on thee in the night watches.

Because thou hast been my help,

therefore in the shadow of thy wings I rejoice.

PSALM 63

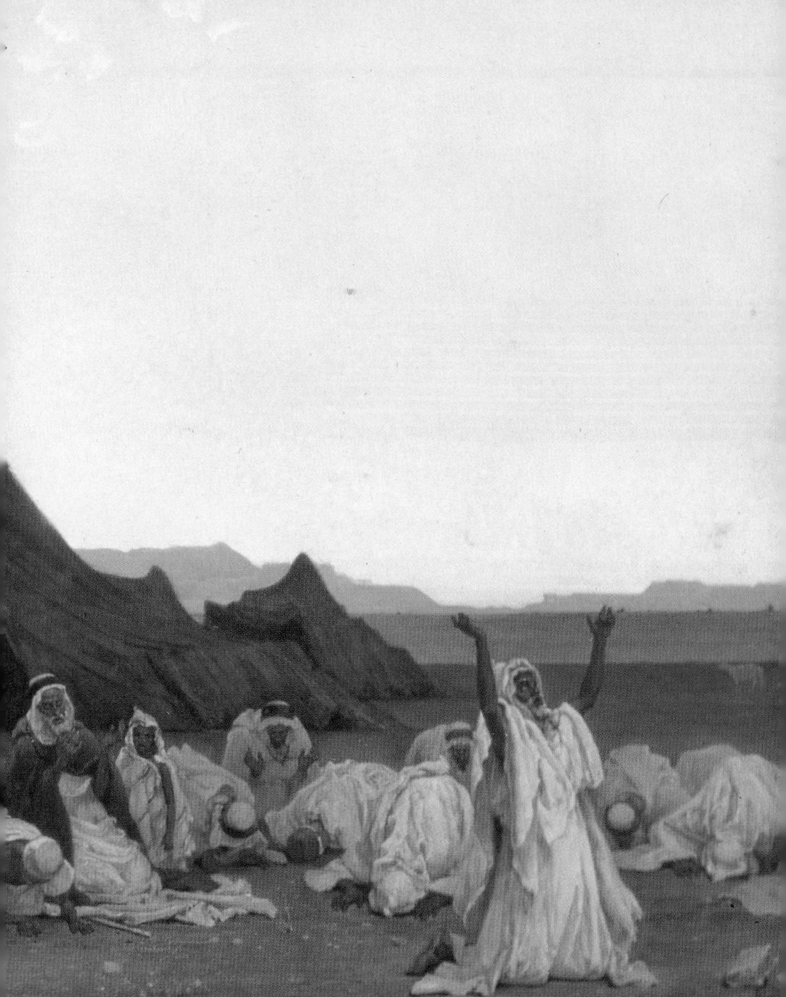

Lawrence of Arabia found much in common with his servant Dahoum. Lawrence was always deeply grateful to him for opening his mind to the solitude of the desert.

He recalls in The Seven Pillars of Wisdom "At last Dahoum drew me: 'Come and smell the very sweetest scent of all,' and we went to the main lodging, to the gaping window sockets of its eastern face, and there drank with open mouths of the effortless, empty, eddyless wind of the desert, throbbing past."

T.E. LAWRENCE

The sun was so hot I was cooking. It was a lonely and exhilarating feeling to see no signs of human hands. No houses, cars, supermarkets, telephone booths. No quick fix in an emergency. Just the cacti rising up against the blue horizon. Some of them twice the size of a man. Some reaching straight up like giant phalluses. Others with two outstretched arms like a human figure. These were my only companions – the men of the desert. I wandered over to one of these burly natives who seemed as permanently angry as the blazing sun. I sat in what little shade there was to drink some water. It was so cool on my throat. I splashed my face – and then it happened. It was as if the great empty sky, my angry cactus friend, and the parched ground beneath me were all shaking with one tremendous pulse of power and a voice, like the voice of the desert, spoke in my ear saying "You are alive!"

STEPHEN ARMSTRONG

Oh that the desert were my dwelling place,

With only one fair spirit for my minister.

That I might all forget the human race,

And hating no one, love her only.

GEORGE GORDON, LORD BYRON

A man can only be free in the desert.

ARAB PROVERB

In the desert
    of the heart,
Let the healing
    fountain start;
In the prison
    of his days,
Teach the free man
    how to praise.

W.H. AUDEN

Go walkabout in the outback then you feel it. You feel it there. We say "djang" – mean energy, power – somethin'. It strong there. You go see like Katatjula – Uluru – other place – sacred place – nice place. You look, but not go there. These day they crawling on Uluru (Ayers Rock) like ants, they don't know why. I don't know why. These places put there in "Tjukurrpa" – Dreamtime – by the Old Ones. Go there with good heart and you feel djang – much power, energy. I'm tellin' you.

BILL BUNGABE

The Nazca Desert is a barren expanse. Flat open nothingness with a shallow overlay of small stones. But the winds are few there and if you kick some of these small stones, where you have walked you will leave your mark for a thousand years. Some years ago someone flew over this desert in a little plane and saw the lines. Long straight lines reaching to the horizon, carefully constructed and clearly delineated. And then the animals – pictures in the desert created by the simple removal of the stones – a monkey, a condor, a spider. The sacred animals of our ancestors, waiting to be seen by someone who flies high enough. Great emblems marked into the very landscape for some magical purpose. Look from the ground and you see nothing. Look from the air and you see everything. I often wonder what our ancestors meant to say to us by this. They had no airplanes. Did these shamans fly up into the sky? What are these mysterious forms? I don't know, but whenever I walk the great spider or dance the lines of the monkey, I feel the blood of my ancient forbears still coursing in my veins and a strange delight fills me.

MARCUS APPOLATIO

There is no sight like the desert night. So many stars I have never seen before. I wandered off from the fire and settled myself onto the back of a dune like a sofa.

I lay down and looked up. There above me was Orion, one of the few constellations that I easily recognize. The ancient Egyptians knew this pattern of stars as the god Osiris — Lord of the Dead. And at his feet is Sirius, the dog star, which they associated with the goddess Isis. The Egyptians believed that each soul is also a star. As I gazed at the plethora of sparkling distant suns I searched for the star that was my soul.

MARTHA KRIPPKE

DESERT THOUGHTS

 THE DESERT is a place of insight. In its uncluttered openness the mind becomes still and empty of distracting chatter, creating space for the quiet spirit. As the Sufi poet Omar Khayyam perceived, in the desert's eternal barrenness we can feel ourselves to be as temporary as snow fallen on the sand. Things appear differently in the desert. What value are all the riches of the world, compared with a single drop of water to slake a parched throat? Life and death stand out more plainly against the clear desert horizon. Under the relentless gaze of the life-giving and life-destroying sun, one is closer to death and more alive.

The worldly hopes men set their hearts upon
Turn ashes — or it prospers; and anon
Like snow upon the desert's dusty face
Lighting a little hour or two — is gone.

Think, in this batter'd Caravanserai
Whose doorways are alternate night and day,
How Sultan after Sultan with his pomp
Abode his hour or two, and went his way.

OMAR KHAYYAM

The sun gives life to
everything;
but in the desert it is the
angel of death.

TRADITIONAL BEDOUIN SAYING

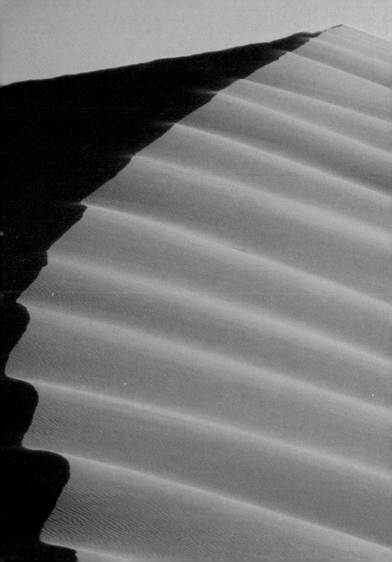

I have driven across the Sahara five times now, and each time I touch death. You need to know what you are doing. One small fault with the truck and you're finished. But if you prepare properly and take precautions it is safer than you might think. Despite this, each year a number of people who try making the crossing will perish in the attempt. The most common reason is following mirages. If they just trusted the compass they would be fine, but seeing what they take to be habitation or an oasis they drive sometimes miles off course and that can be fatal. I have often mused about this as I've driven over that dusty expanse. It increasingly feels to me that if I could stop following mirages in my life I might get less lost in the turmoil of anxiety that has plagued me since I was a child. I guess that for some people the idea of crossing the Sahara is fearful and intimidating. For me it is inspiring and refreshing. When I cross the desert I've got a map and a compass – for the rest of my life I have neither and end up simply following mirages.

HUGH HOLGER

All sunshine makes a desert.

ARAB PROVERB

It is the sandstorms that shape the stone statues of the desert.
It is the struggles of life that form a person's character.

NATIVE AMERICAN PROVERB

Fear Allah like a sandstorm.

BEDOUIN SAYING

In the desert water is worth more than gold.

ARAB PROVERB

Many desert stories are told to account for particular features of the landscape. One such is told of Sheik Hadji Abdul-Aziz, a Sufi dervish. He was traveling through a desert one summer in stifling sun. Parched and fatigued he spotted a beautiful green garden, full of fruit. He called to the gardener,

> *"My fellow man, in the name of Allah the merciful, give me a melon and I will give you my prayers." The gardener replied, "I'm not interested in your prayers, give me your money." The dervish answered, "But I am a beggar and have no money. I am sweating and thirsty, all I need is one of your melons." The gardener rebuffed him again saying, "Well go to the Nile and drink there." So the*

dervish lifted his eyes to heaven and prayed,

"O Allah, You who quenched the thirst of Ismail

by creating the fountain of Zem-Zem in the midst

of the desert, will you allow one of your creatures

to die of thirst?"

Hardly had these words left his lips than a gentle

dew began to fall, refreshing his weary body.

After this miracle the gardener knew he was in

the presence of a holy man loved by Allah, and

he quickly offered him one of his melons. Hadji

Abdul-Aziz rebuffed him saying, "Keep it foolish

man. Your melons will become as hard as your

heart and this garden as barren as your soul."

Right away the melons turned to blocks of

stone and the land to sand – the very stones and

sand that can be seen at that spot to this day.

A greedy Caliph was very attached to his wealth, so the Sufi sage Shaqiq asked him, "Would you give one half of your kingdom to someone who could provide you with a drink of water if you were in the desert dying of thirst?" The Caliph said he would. Shaqiq then asked "Would you give the other half of your kingdom to someone able to help you pass that water if you had become unable to do so?" The Caliph again agreed that he would. "Why then do you value your kingdom so highly," asked Shaqiq, "when you would give it away in return for a drink of water which would itself not even stay with you?"

SUFI TEACHING STORY

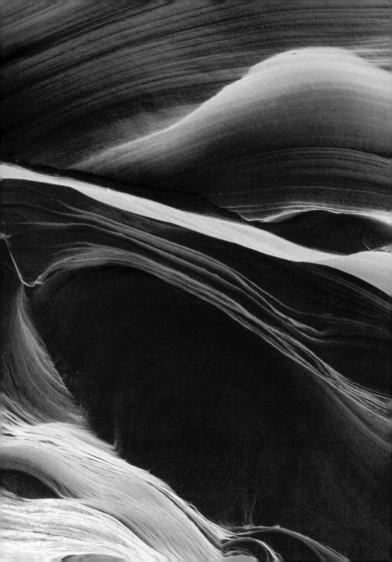

WISDOM OF THE WILDERNESS

 THE GOSPEL OF MATTHEW describes Jesus being led into the desert to be tested by the Devil. Going alone into the wilderness to find God and face your demons is an ancient spiritual tradition that is still practiced in shamanic cultures throughout the world. Native Americans, for example, practice the Vision Quest in which a quester will fast and pray alone in a remote and wild location for a number of days. During this time, he or she will receive visions and be spiritually tested. Being isolated in the desert is a lonely and life-threatening undertaking. The spiritual seeker who voluntarily undergoes such an ordeal is choosing to face his or her fear of death and solitude in a direct and powerfully transformative way.

Jesus was led by the spirit into the desert to be tempted by the Devil. After forty days and forty nights he was very hungry. The tempter appeared to him and said, "If you are the Son of God magically change these stones into loaves of bread." Jesus replied "The scripture teaches 'Man shall not live by bread alone, but by every word from the mouth of God.'"

Then the Devil took him to a holy city and placed him on a high pinnacle. "If you are the Son of God," he said, "then throw yourself off. For scripture says 'He will charge his angels with protecting you and they will bear you up in case you should dash your foot against a stone.'" Jesus replied "Yes that is true, but scripture also says 'You should not tempt the Lord your God.'"

After this the Devil took him to a high mountain from which could be seen the magnificence of all the kingdoms of the world. "I will give you all of this," he said "if you fall down and worship me." Jesus replied "Away with you Satan! Scripture says 'You shall worship the Lord your God and serve only Him.'"

Then the Devil left Jesus alone and angels came to him and took care of him.

THE GOSPEL OF MATTHEW

The Gnostics were early Christian heretics who inhabited the Egyptian deserts. Some of their lost gospels were discovered in 1945 hidden in a cave at Nag Hammadi in Upper Egypt. One text, called Zostrianos, relates how a spiritual master attained enlightenment. First he removed all physical desires and calmed the "chaos in the mind" with meditation. He then tells us, "After I had set myself straight, I had a vision of the perfect child." Following this experience of the divine presence he wandered out into the desert, half expecting to be killed by wild animals. Here he finally received a vision of "the Messenger of the Knowledge of the Eternal Light." He encourages us, "Why are you hesitating? Seek when you are sought. When you are invited, listen. Look at the Light. Do not be led astray to your destruction."

ZOSTRIANOS

In the old days, when a man went out to get visions – to the wilderness, or a high place, a desert, somewhere all alone – well then, in the old days he didn't know if he would ever come back again. He found that place and made a circle in the sand, then he sat in the circle and waited for visions. Days and nights with no food and just a blanket – now after some time the vision comes. He smokes the sacred tobacco and prays and he is singing all his heart to the Great Spirit, saying "Give me a vision." He gets very scared out there. But his medicine protects him until the vision comes.

ROLLING THUNDER

*A man finds out who
he is in the wilderness.
His soul speaks to him.*

JAMES RUNNING DEER

When a Cleverman go to the outback, he not takin' a holiday you know. He healin' somethin' or someone. Healin' some person, like curin' sick person. So listen me story. I'm tellin'. Cleverman go out where nothin' livin'. But he livin'. He not laughin'. He gonna make rain or somethin'. He all alone but really he not there. He some place else. Dreamin' some place. He know what he doin' alright.

BILL BUNGABE

*T*he Sufis revere Jesus as a great prophet. They
know him as "Issa son of Miryam," and tell
teaching stories that reveal his wisdom. In the New
Testament when Jesus is tested by the Devil, he wisely
resists the temptation to use his magical powers. A Sufi
teaching story relates what happens to some of his
disciples who were not so wise.

Issa was walking in the desert near Jerusalem with his followers who begged him to tell them the secret Name by which he had the power to raise the dead. He said, "If I tell you, you won't use it wisely." They replied, "We are ready Master and it will strengthen our faith." "You don't know what you are asking," he told them. They insisted, however, so reluctantly he revealed to them the secret Name. A little later these people left Issa and came upon a heap of whitened bones. "Let's try out that magic Name," one of them suggested. Immediately they did so, the bones became clothed with flesh and were transformed into a wild beast that tore them all to shreds. Such is the danger of knowledge without the wisdom to use it.

SUFI TEACHING STORY

The Sufis believe that there is no universal right way to approach God, and that each seeker must follow the dictates of his or her own heart. This moral is brought out by the Sufi master Jalaludin Rumi in an amusing tale about another desert prophet, the Jewish leader Moses. In the Bible, Moses hears God speak to him from a burning bush while he is leading the Jewish people out of exile in Egypt across the desert to the Promised Land. At that time God reveals himself as a grand lawgiver who presents Moses with the Ten Commandments. In this Sufi story, however, God presents a friendly, compassionate face, and rebukes Moses for his spiritual grandiosity.

One day Moses came across a humble old shepherd in the desert, who was privately talking to God. The shepherd's tone was relaxed and familiar. He told God how he wanted to help Him: to pick the lice off of Him; to wash His clothes; to kiss His feet and hands. He ended his prayer with "When I think of You all I can say is Ahhhhh!" Moses was appalled and exclaimed "Do you realize that you are talking to the Creator of Heaven and Earth, not to your old uncle?!" The shepherd felt very foolish and asked Moses if he thought God would ever forgive him. However, as the shepherd began to wander off sadly into the desert to repent, a divine voice spoke to Moses rebuking him.

"Moses, what to you seems wrong is right to him. One man's poison is another man's honey. Purity and impurity, sloth and diligence – what do these matter to me? I am above all that. Ways of worship can not be put in ranks as better or worse. It is all praise and it is all right. It is the worshiper who is glorified by worship – not I. I don't listen to the words. I look inside at the humility. Only that low and open emptiness is real. Forget language – I want burning, burning! Be friends with this fire. Burn up your grand ideas and special words!"

JALALUDIN RUMI

A man knocked on a door. "Who's there?" asked God. "Me" replied the man. "Go away then," said God. The man left and wandered in the arid desert until he realized his error. He returned to the door and knocked again. "Who's there?" asked God. "You," replied the man. "Then come in," said God, "There's no room here for two."

SUFI TEACHING STORY

DESERT FATHERS

THE MOST FAMOUS of all desert mystics are the early Christian recluses who made their homes in solitary caves or small communities out in the wildernesses of the Middle East – earning themselves the name of the "Desert Fathers". Their title of "Abba" means simply "Father". One of their centers was called Cellia because of the number of cells scattered around the desert. This environment was utterly desolate and the cells were so separated that no one could see or hear his neighbor. In this huge quiet these mystics prayed, fasted, and received their visions. The Desert Fathers were called "anchorites" meaning "rule-breakers" because they had abandoned all their public duties. Their lives were hard and simple, yet from this crude existence came a capacity for kindness and wisdom.

Abba Zeno said, "If someone wants to be heard by God, then before he prays for his own soul, or for anything else, let him pray with all his heart for his enemies. If he does this God will hear everything he asks."

Amma Syncletica said "At first those who are going towards God experience great battles and much suffering, but afterwards ineffable joy. It is like lighting a fire. To begin with you get choked with smoke and end up crying. For, as it is written, 'Our God is a consuming fire.'"

Abba Lot said to Abba Joseph, "I fast, I pray, I meditate. As far as I can I purify my thoughts. What else can I do?" Abba Joseph stretched out his old hands toward heaven and his fingers became like lamps of light. He said, "If you will it, you can become all fire."

A brother was talking to Abba Matoes about the virtue of loving one's enemies. Abba Matoes replied, "As for myself, I have yet to manage truly to love those that love me."

Blessed Anthony was praying one day when a voice said, "Anthony, you are still not of the stature of the tanner in the city." So Anthony went to find the tanner and said to him, "I have left the desert to find you. Please tell me about your good works." The tanner replied, "I am not aware of having done any good works. When I get up, before I start work, I affirm that the whole of this city, great and small, will go to the kingdom of God, while I alone will go to eternal punishment for the evil in my heart. That is all." Anthony said, "You work in the city with all its distractions while I sit in solitude in the desert, but I have not come near the wisdom of these words."

Abba Macarius was praying in his cell in the desert when a hyena appeared and began to lick his feet. Gently dragging the edge of his tunic, she pulled him toward her cave. Inside were her cubs, which had been born blind. Abba Macarius prayed over them and their sight was healed. By way of thanks the hyena brought him a huge ram skin and laid it at his feet. He smiled as if at a kindly person and spread the skin under him to give a prayer of thanksgiving.

A hunter in the desert came across Abba Anthony and
the brothers playing and laughing. He was shocked and
disapproving. Abba Anthony said to him, "Put an arrow
in your bow and shoot it." The hunter did so and Abba
Anthony said, "And now another." He did so, but Anthony
demanded, "Now one more." The hunter exclaimed, "If I
bend my bow too much it will break." Then old Anthony
said, "It is like that with God's work. If I stretch the brothers
too much they will break. Sometimes it is necessary to relax."

A hermit who could cast out demons asked
them, "Is it fasting that gives me the power
    to banish you?"
The demons replied, "We do not eat."
He asked, "Is it my long vigils?"
The demons replied, "We do not sleep."
He asked, "Is it retreat from the world?"
The demons replied, "We live in the deserts."
He asked, "What is it, then, that gives me
    power over you?"
The demons replied, "Nothing can overcome us
    but humility."

AMMA THEODORA

A brother asked Abba Peomen, "How should I behave in my desert cell?" Abba Peomen replied, "Wherever you live, live like a stranger and do not expect your words to have any influence, then you will be at peace."

The Way of
THE SEA

INTRODUCTION

It is a deeply spiritual experience to stand by the sea and sense its power; to see it stretching to the horizon and be awed by its scope and beauty. The immense oceans clothe the Earth. From outer space ours is a blue planet. Is it more than a remarkable coincidence that the percentage of our home world covered by the seas is the same as the percentage of water in a human body? We are water beings. To commune with the sea is to experience the primal home of all life forms, from which all creatures have evolved.

Yet the sea is mighty and fearful. It is the tomb of countless anonymous adventures. It rages and gales. Its water cannot quench our thirst. Its depths are dark and secret places. We know more about the moon than these unfathomable worlds. We have crossed the oceans but have not tamed them. The sea is still wild. Perhaps that is why to stand by her shores, where the winds blow and the spume hisses, is to feel truly free; to know that we will pass like the crashing waves and another will rise behind us, while the tides roll in and out for all eternity.

THE MYSTICAL SEA

THE VAST OCEAN is a perennial image of the all
encompassing nature of God. The great Hindu mystic
Sankara described Brahman, the ineffable Oneness of God, as an
ocean of endless joy. The Ashtavakra Gita, a Hindu scripture, points
toward our essential shared identity as the Atman – a limitless sea
of Being on which individual selves rise and fall like waves. The
Buddha compares the experience of enlightenment to a drop of
water merging with the sea from which it came. The Taoist Lao
Tzu sees himself on a journey back to the Tao, the primal Source,
like a river rushing to the sea. Yet these images do not suffice to
convey the sublime nature of the Truth the mystics have experi-
enced. Like the frog in a traditional Hindu teaching story, all the
mystics can ultimately do is encourage us to experience the ocean
of God for ourselves.

Following Tao in the world
is as natural as a mountain stream,
that becomes part of a valley brook,
that becomes part of a great river,
that flows to the One Sea.

LAO TZU

As rivers flow into the sea
and in so doing lose name and form,
so the wise, who are free from name and form,
reach the Supreme Being,
the Self-luminous, the Infinite.
Someone who knows Brahman
becomes Brahman.

MUNDAKA UPANISHAD

Streams and rivers flow to the sea,
    because it lies below them.
That's why it is the greatest body of water.
Following this example,
    the wise are always humble.

LAO TZU

My mind fell like a hailstone into the vast expanse of Brahman's ocean. Touching one drop of it, I melted away and became one with Brahman. This is wonderful indeed! Here is the ocean of Brahman, full of endless joy. How can I accept or reject anything? Is there anything distinct from Brahman? Now, finally and clearly, I know that I am the Atman, the One Soul, whose nature is eternal bliss. I see nothing. I hear nothing. I know nothing that is separate from me.

SANKARA

I am the breathing wind

and the ocean waves.

I am the sun's bright rays,

and the sparkling stars.

I am the rustling leaves,

and the power that brings

the bud into blossom.

I am the salmon swimming,

the brave boar fighting,

the fast stag running,

the strong ox pulling,

the mighty oak standing.

I am the thoughts of everyone,

who praises my exquisite beauty.

THE CELTIC CHRISTIAN
BLACK BOOK OF CARMARTHEN

O, the wonder that I am! I salute myself who, though with a body, am one who neither goes anywhere nor comes from anywhere but ever abides pervading the universe.

O, in Me the limitless ocean! The movement of the mind has produced the many worlds like the wind produces diverse waves on the ocean.

How remarkable! In Me the limitless ocean. The waves of individual selves rise according to their inherent nature, meet and play with one another for a while and then disappear.

ASHTAVAKRA GITA

The cycle of reincarnation is like the water cycle.
Water evaporates into nothingness and then falls as droplets
from the heavens, like the individual souls incarnating here
on earth – only to make their way via streams and rivers to
the mighty sea, and to be evaporated once again by the
great spiritual sun into nothingness.

SHEN HSUI

All the rivers run into the sea,
yet it is not full;
unto the place from whence the rivers run,
thither they return again.

ECCLESIASTES

A toad who lived in a well was one day visited by a toad who lived in the sea. "How big is your well?" asked the first toad. "Is it as big as mine?" The sea toad smiled and tried to explain, "My well is so huge that it has no edges. It contains so much water that it could never run dry in a million hot summers. It is so deep that perhaps it has no bottom." The first toad looked incredulous. "You are either boasting or your imagination has run away with itself!" he complained. "Come with me," said the sea toad, "and I will show you."

HINDU TEACHING STORY

What am I? What are you? We are all aspects of the one sea of Being. Our lives are the rising and falling of a passing wave on the eternal ocean which, in truth, we are.

ISSA DAS

Don't think that saying "I am God" is proclaiming one's greatness. It is actually total humility. Someone who says "I am the servant of God" infers two – God and himself – whereas someone who says "I am God" negates himself. He relinquishes his own existence. "I am God" means "I don't exist. Everything is God. Only God exists. I am nothing. I am utter emptiness." This is complete humility not arrogance, but people often misunderstand. When someone says that he is God's servant, he still sees himself as a "doer", albeit in God's service. He is not yet drowned in the ocean of God. When he is, there will be no such thing as " his actions," only movements of the water.

JALALUDIN RUMI

The liberated soul loses her name in the One

through Whom and in Whom she merges;

just as a river reaching the sea

loses the identity with which it flowed

through many countries

to arrive at this destination.

Now it is in the sea

and here it rests without labor.

MARGUERITE PORETE

*H*is will is the ocean into which

all streams and currents pour.

ALIGHIERI DANTE

Time is like a bubble on the ocean of eternity. Before the bubble was in existence the ocean was there, and after the bubble bursts the ocean will be there still.

DR. CHRISTIE

You are a droplet of water from an infinite
ocean of consciousness.

HAJI BAHAUDIN

THE SPIRITUAL SEA

THE SEA is a teacher with much wisdom to impart.

Like life itself, she washes all before her. She speaks with many voices: the low growl of the breakers on the rock; the gentle hiss as she caresses soft sand; the mournful cry of her seagulls; the thunderous cacophony of her angry storms. Each voice has spoken to some witness of the grandeur and depths of life, of immortality; of a power more permanent than our own transitory existence. What greater reminder is there of the awesome mystery that surrounds us everywhere than the endless sea, playfully splashing and murderously raging?

He that will learn to pray, let him go to the sea.

GEORGE HERBERT

They that go down to the sea in ships,

that do business in great waters;

these see the works of the Lord,

and his wonders in the deep.

PSALM 107

Now I perceive that I have not understood anything –

not a single object – and that no man ever can.

I perceive Nature, here in sight of the sea, is taking advantage

of me, to dart upon me, and sting me,

Because I have dared to open my mouth and sing at all.

WALT WHITMAN

God alone can fully and always hear the voice that the earth utters to the sky the many tongues of its many waters. But He sends us men sometimes to whom He has given such ears in their soul that they can perceive some of the meaning of the world's great sea voice, and they are able to translate for us some of the music and the magic of the sea-soul of the earth. These men are poets or painters, or musicians, and they can hear more than most of us, far more than we hear at the coast, of the great sea's musical mystery, the strange trouble of the weird waters, and the moving ocean's mighty joy. And they sing for us, these men, what the sea says, and their voice is beautiful and wonderful.

J.P. FORSYTH

Thou paragon of elemental powers,

Mystery of water – never slumbering sea!

Impassioned orator with lips sublime,

Whose waves are arguments which prove a God!

ROBERT MONTGOMERY

Hence in a season of calm weather,

Though inland far we be,

Our souls have sight of that immortal sea,

Which brought us hither,

Can in a moment travel thither,

And hear the mighty waters rolling evermore.

WILLIAM WORDSWORTH

As I wend to the shores I know not,

As I list to the dirge, the voices of men and
women wrecked,

As I inhale the impalpable breezes that set in
upon me,

As the ocean so mysterious rolls towards me
closer and closer,

I too but signify, at the utmost, a little
washed-up drift,

A few sands and dead leaves to gather,

Gather, and merge myself as part of the
sands and drift.

WALT WHITMAN

Those overtaken by a storm when traveling by sea don't worry about their luggage, but throw it overboard with their own hands, considering their property to be less important than their lives. So why don't we, following their example, throw out whatever drags our soul down to the depths.

ST. NELIOS THE ASCETIC

The sea reflects the sun perfectly if the water is still. But if it is agitated by the wind the light fragments into a million mirrored suns. It is like this with the mind. If the mind is disturbed by thoughts, the Light of Oneness is fragmented and we perceive only the manyness of things. When thoughts are still, however, the One Light is perfectly reflected in the mind.

ISSA DAS

Imagine an ox's yoke adrift on the vast ocean
and a turtle happening to poke its head
through the hole – this is how rare and extra-
ordinary it is to be born a human being.

KUNKYEN LONGCHEN RABJAM

If you would swim on the bosom
of the ocean of Truth,
you must reduce yourself to a zero.

MAHATMA GANDHI

*I*n China there once lived a wrestler called "Great Waves." He was immensely strong and in practice sessions always won his contests. But in public he always failed. Great Waves went to Hakuju, a Zen master, for help. The master advised, "Great Waves" is your name, so stay in the temple tonight and imagine that you are the huge billowing sea, swallowing all in its path — unstoppable!" The wrestler meditated all night in the temple. At first he was distracted, but gradually he saw himself as a mighty wave — becoming larger and larger. Soon the shrine and the statue of the Buddha were swept away before him — the whole temple became the ebb and flow of the sea. In the morning Hakuju found him faintly smiling. He patted the wrestler on the shoulders and said, "You are those waves. You will sweep all before you." After that no wrestler could ever defeat Great Waves.

ZEN TEACHING STORY

The ancient philosopher Diagoras the Cynic was admiring with a friend the many votive monuments to the gods surrounding a temple. His friend explained to him that these structures had been erected out of gratitude by those who, whilst in peril on the sea, had promised to honor the gods if divine intervention rescued them from a watery grave. The monuments were testimony to the efficacy of prayer and the power of the gods. Diagoras replied sardonically, "Just think how many more there would have been if all those who had drowned had also been able to set one up."

CICERO

Diagoras was on a voyage when the sea became very rough. The nervous crew began muttering that it was because they were carrying on board someone who ridiculed the gods as religious superstition. Pointing out other ships also caught in the same storm, Diagoras muttered, "How remarkable! If you are right, every one of these vessels must also be carrying a Diagoras as a passenger."

CICERO

Love still has something
of the sea.

SIR CHARLES SIDNEY

OCEAN OF LOVE

THE MANY MOODS of the ocean have offered poets a
constant source of evocative imagery for the life of the
passions – especially love. Whether it be love of another or ecstatic
love of God, poets and mystics turn to metaphors of the sea to
express their obsessive ardor. Aphrodite, the Greek goddess of love
and desire, was born from the sea. She rose naked from the spume
riding a scallop shell and was known as "the foam-born." She came
from the chaos and danced on the shores. To experience the love
she inspires is to be lost in an ocean of bliss. To be abandoned by
love is to feel adrift in a small boat, tossed by currents beyond any
control. Our emotions, like the ocean, are delightful and destruc-
tive. But without them it would be a dry world.

The bridegroom sea
Is toying with the shore, his wedded bride,
And in the fullness of his marriage joy
He decorates her tawny brow with shells,
Retires a pace to see how fair she looks,
Then, proud, runs up to kiss her.

ALEXANDER SMITH

Unchangeable, save to thy wild wave's play;

Time writes no wrinkle on thine azure brow,

Such as creation's dawn beheld, thou rollest now.

Thou glorious mirror, where the Almighty's form

Glasses itself in tempests, in all time,

Calm or convulsed, in breeze, or gale, or storm,

Icing the pole, or in the torrid clime,

Dark-heaving – boundless, endless, and sublime,

The image of eternity, the throne

Of the Invisible; even from out thy slime

The monsters of the deep are made; each zone

Obeys thee; thou goest forth, dread, fathomless, alone.

And I have loved thee, Ocean!

GEORGE GORDON, LORD BYRON

Soothe! soothe! soothe!

Close on each wave soothes the wave behind,

And again another behind, embracing and
            lapping, everyone close –

But my love soothes not me, not me.

Low hangs the moon – it rose late;

O it is lagging – O I think it is heavy with
            love, with love.

O madly the sea pushes, pushes upon
            the land, with love – with love.

O night! do I not see my love fluttering out there
            amongst the breakers?

What is that little black thing I see there in the white?

Loud! loud! loud!

Loud I call to you, my love!

High and clear I shoot my voice over the waves;

Surely you must know who is here, is here;

You must know who I am, my love.

WALT WHITMAN

My tossing mind
becomes becalmed
as you walk
across its waters.

ISSA DAS

My soul is an enchanted boat,

Which like a sleeping swan, doth float,

upon the silver waves of thy sweet singing.

PERCY BYSSHE SHELLEY

I navigate serious seas

only soothed by your smile.

Be my lifeboat

and my star to guide it.

Only you can bring me home,

for you are where my heart is.

ISSA DAS

Many waves cannot quench love,
Nor can the flood drown it out.

THE SONG OF SOLOMON

Like as the waves make towards the pebbled shore

    So do our minutes hasten to their end;

Each changing place with that which goes before,

    In sequent toil all forwards do contend.

Nativity, once in the main of light,

    Crawls to maturity, wherewith being crowned,

Crooked eclipses 'gainst his glory fight,

    And Time that gave doth now his gift confound.

Time doth transfix the flourish set on youth

    And delves the parallels in beauty's brow,

Feeds on the rarities of nature's truth,

    And nothing stands but for his scythe to mow.

      And yet to time in hope my verse shall stand,

      Praising thy worth, despite his cruel hand.

WILLIAM SHAKESPEARE

One day I wrote her name upon the sand,

But came the waves and washed it away.

Again I wrote it with a second hand,

But came in the sand and made my

pains his prey. Vain man said she, that

dost vain assay, a mortal thing so to immortalize.

EMILY DICKINSON

*The milky way is as flotsam
on the vast ocean of ecstatic love.*

JALALUDIN RUMI

Imagine Brahman as a sea without shores. Through the cooling love of the devotee some of the water becomes frozen into blocks of ice. Now and then, God assumes a form and reveals Himself to his lovers as a person. But when the sun of Knowledge rises the blocks of ice melt away and God is without form, no more a person. He is beyond description. Who could describe Him? Anyone who tries disappears, unable to find his "I" anymore.

RAMAKRISHNA

Chained by love.
Captured again.
Struggle is futile.
Escape is impossible.

Love is a sea
with unseen shores —
with no shores at all.
The wary don't dive in.
To swim in love
is to drink poison
and find it sweet.

I struggled like a wild mare
drawing the noose tighter.

RABI'A

*M*y brimming heart
held whole in full embrace,
flotsam upon the tides of breath,
washed in taste, splashed by spume of light,
tossed by Tao's undulant pulse,
born on swells of simple love,
falling into waiting arms,
surging up from depths of bliss.

Eroded by the turmoil of your ocean presence,
waves of ringing break on rough rocks,
sucking back smooth pebbles,
grinding grit to soft sand,
dissolving my grateful heart in your bounty.

ISSA DAS

Why should we ever part – we two?

Like the leaves of a plant floating on the waters –

we live as the Great One and the small one.

Like the owl gazing all night at the moon –

We live as the Great One and the small one.

This love cannot end –

it goes back to the very first lovers.

This is what Kabir says:

Just as river water becomes sea water,

You and I are indivisible.

KABIR

If all the land were turned to paper
and all the seas to ink,
and all the forests into pens to write with,
they would still not suffice
to describe the greatness of the guru.

KABIR

SEA OF IMAGES

 THE GREAT PSYCHOLOGIST Carl Jung compared the "collective unconscious" to the sea. To dream of the sea is to encounter the hidden depths we share. The ocean contains images, as rich as sunken treasure, that question and inform our terrestrial existence. Her metaphors are as fluid as her currents, defying the limitations of the rational mind and exciting the poetic imagination. To some she whispers "life" to others "death" yet contained in both is the silent message "mystery". Her roar drowns out the chatter of the trivial mind, and in that white noise can be heard the secret silence of the soul.

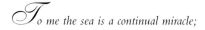

To me the sea is a continual miracle;

The fishes that swim

— the rocks

— the motion of the waves

— the ships with men in them,

What stranger miracles are there?

WALT WHITMAN

One bright morning in mid-ocean I looked off upon the water and it was so calm and bright I said "This is the infinite smile of an infinite God." Then again in the summer time, strolling near the beach in the darkness, I heard the voice of the waters, and I said, "This is the long metre psalm of the deep."

TALMAGE

It is not by descriptions

that the magic of the sea

can be brought before the reader's mind.

This can only be achieved

by the unconscious touch

of one between whom and the sea

there exists a sympathy

as rare as it is mysterious.

There are but few who know

how the beauty of every other object of nature

is increased and intensified

as soon as ever it touches the sea.

There are but few who really feel

how the joyful news of sunrise,

is never fully and finally proclaimed

till the sea has owned it,

caught it, tossed it from wave to wave.

There are but few who really feel

that the silent message of the moon

is never so eloquent in its silence

as when translated by the rippling disk

that answers it in the bosom of the sea.

There are few that really feel

that the calm stars are never so full

with comfort to a soul in sorrow,

and that the bright cloud-pageantry

of a summer noon is never so joyful

to a soul in joy, as when all these riches

of the earth and air live a larger and fuller life

in the mirror that girdles the world.

ATHEOUM

Some people call the great world God's cathedral.

Well one of its organs is the sea.

Oh it is a great organ the sea!

It can play as sweet and soft as a flute.

But it can also roar and thunder to terrify the bravest.

It is awful to hear the sea rolling in like mountains

upon a shore of rocks and caves,

and rousing echoes which are heard far inland

as if many giants were roaring into many tunes.

I suppose it is very silent at the bottom of the sea.

The fishes and the shells may know nothing

of all the concert amid which they live.

But we can hear it, though we can hardly tell the words it sings.

We can hear its music, so strange,

mysterious, magical, and mighty.

There are some hearts it can speak to, and they know what it says.

They listen and they are soothed;

or they listen and they feel something like rapture;

or as they listen they feel something like terror,

but always they love as they listen

to the many sounds and the one great voice.

REV. P.T. FORSYTH

The world is too much with us; late and soon,

Getting and spending, we lay waste our powers,

Little we see in Nature which is ours;

We have given our hearts away, a sordid boon!

This sea that bares her bosom to the moon;

The winds that will be howling at all hours,

And are up-gathered now like sleeping flowers;

For this, for everything, we are out of tune;

It moves us not, Great God! I'd rather be

A Pagan suckled in a creed outworn;

So might I, standing on this pleasant lea,

Have glimpses that would make me less forlorn;

Have sight of Proteus coming from the sea;

Or hear old Triton blow his wreathed horn.

WILLIAM WORDSWORTH

There is a tide in the affairs of men,

Which, taken at the flood, leads on to fortune;

Omitted, all the voyage of their life,

Is bound in shallows, and in miseries:

And we must take the current when it serves,

Or lose our ventures.

WILLIAM SHAKESPEARE

The sea is the largest of all cemeteries,

and its slumberers sleep without monuments.

All other graveyards, in all other lands,

show some symbol of distinction

between the great and the small, the rich and poor;

but in that ocean cemetery, the king and the clown,

the prince and the peasant, are alike distinguished.

The same waves roll over all, the same requiem

by the minstrels of the ocean is sung to their honor.

Over their remains the same storm beats,

and the same sun shines; and there, unmarked,

the weak and the powerful, the plumed and the unhonored,

will sleep on until awakened by the same trump,

when the sea shall give up its dead.

MANTELL

The dim, dark sea,
so like unto Death,
That divides and yet
unites mankind!

HENRY WADSWORTH LONGFELLOW

Whereto answering the sea,

delaying not, hurrying not,

Whispered me through the night,

      and very plainly before daybreak,

Lisped to me the low and delicious word DEATH;

And again Death – ever Death, Death, Death,

Hissing melodious, neither like the bird

      nor like my aroused child's heart,

But edging near, as privately for me, rustling at my feet,

creeping thence steadily up to my ears,

      and loving me softly all over,

Death, Death, Death, Death, Death.

My own songs awakened from that hour;

And with them the key, the word up from the waves,

The word of the sweetest song, and all songs,

That strong and delicious word which, creeping to my feet,

The Sea whispered me.

WALT WHITMAN

127

Library of Congress Cataloging-in-Publication Data Available

10 9 8 7 6 5 4 3 2 1

Published in 2001 by Sterling Publishing Company, Inc.
387 Park Avenue South, New York, N.Y. 10016

Originally published separately in 1998 as
The Way of the Desert and *The Way of the Sea*.

© 1998, 2001 GODSFIELD PRESS

Text © 1998 Timothy Freke

Produced for Sterling Publishing by
Godsfield Press Limited

Designed by the
Bridgewater Book Company

Distributed in Canada by Sterling Publishing
c/o Canadian Manda Group, One Atlantic Avenue, Suite 105
Toronto, Ontario, Canada M6K 3E7

Distributed in Australia by Capricorn Link (Australia) Pty Ltd
P O. Box 6651, Baulkham Hills, Business Centre, NSW 2153, Australia

Printed and bound in China

ISBN 0-8069-2511-6

The publisher would like to thank that following for the use of pictures:

Fine Art Photographic Library, The Stock Market

Author's Acknowledgments

My thanks to Deborah O'Shea, and Ellen and John Freke,
for all their help in compiling this little book.